JACOB –
WRESTLER FOR GOD

Stephanie Jeffs

Other titles in this series by Stephanie Jeffs
Joshua – warrior for God
Elijah – champion for God
Peter – fisherman for God

Copyright © Stephanie Jeffs 2001
First published 2001

Scripture Union, 207–209 Queensway, Bletchley,
Milton Keynes, MK2 2EB, England.

ISBN 1 85999 444 X

British Library Cataloguing-in-Publication Data.
A catalogue record of this book is available from the British
Library.

Printed and bound in Great Britain by Creative Print and
Design (Wales) Ebbw Vale.

Chapter One

I can't stand my brother! Do you know what I mean?

It's a shame really, because we're twins. But we're not identical. No way! I haven't got anything much in common with him. He's big and hairy. And I'm, well, smaller, but I'm not short. Just about right. And I haven't got hairy arms. Yuk! Esau's gross! He's so big and hairy. And he fancies himself.

"You'd never believe you were twins," my mother, Rebecca is always saying.

She's right. You never would. Esau loves being outside all the time. He thinks he's really fit and cool. He's always going off with his bow and arrow, trying to hunt some weird animal or something. What a waste of time. I mean, it isn't as though we're short of animals where we live. My dad, Isaac, has loads. He owns hundreds of goats and sheep. They're all over the place.

When we were little, Esau and I used to fight all the time. It was terrible. Mum says

3

we were scrapping before we were born. And she should know! But now we're older we just stay away from each other, as much as we can. But even so, he still annoys me. He's always having a go. "We may be twins, but I'm still the oldest," he says. Only just! When he was born, I was hanging onto his foot!

Anyway, the worst thing about it is that because Esau's the eldest, he gets all the special treatment, all the things that eldest sons get and I won't! He'll be the head of the family, and he'll get a far bigger share of the inheritance than me when Dad dies. And even before that happens, Dad will give him a special blessing. You know the sort of thing – Dad'll put his hands on Esau and ask God to give him loads of good stuff – the sort of things everybody wants, but you can only have if it's your "birthright" as the elder son.

That's never going to happen to me! More's the pity! Know the reason why? Because I am younger than him. Just because I was born a few minutes after Esau.

Dad thinks Esau's great. Well, I suppose they both like the same things. Noise, exercise, hunting, bloodand guts – you know the sort of things. I prefer staying at home. Anyway, I've never liked tramping across the open countryside. And because I prefer to stay at home, Esau calls me "Mummy's boy!" Huh! He makes me really mad sometimes!

The kind of life we live, there's always something to do back at the tents, and plenty of people around. Actually, one of the things I like to do is cook. I try and use fresh ingredients, not the salted stuff, and I love to use different herbs and colours. One of my favourites is lentil stew. I know! Lentil stew sounds unexciting, boring even, something you can eat any old day. But then you haven't tasted my lentil stew, have you?

One day, I had made a really good fire and filled the best cooking pot full of water. While I was waiting for the water to boil, I started to pod some lentils. They smelled great. I sprinkled them into the water, and then I started to chop up the other ingredients: onions, leeks, garlic and mint. Delicious! I broke up some salt and put that in too. Before long the water had turned a thick bubbly red. Everyone was sniffing the

air as they walked past the pot. I just kept
stirring and adding the odd sprig of dill. It's
really worth taking your time over lentil
stew.

Well, as I was quietly minding my own
business, stirring the stew, Esau came up to
me. He was absolutely filthy, covered in
mud, and his hands were red with blood.
He was all sweaty, too. Disgusting. I
thought he was going to drip something
revolting into my stew.

"Give me some stew, Jake," he said. He
always calls me Jake when he wants some-

thing. He rubbed his hand across his forehead and smeared mud everywhere. He's such a slob!

I didn't say anything.

"Please, Jake," he begged. "I've been out hunting all day. I'm starving. Go on. Please give me some. You know how much I like your lentil stew."

Liar! I've never heard him say before how much he liked my lentil stew.

"Please!" he whined.

I'd never heard him whine before, either. Normally he just takes what he wants and doesn't bother to ask.

Suddenly I had a really great idea. A brainwave! It was pretty sneaky, actually.

"Have some," I said. I got hold of a bowl and ladled some in. I looked at Esau's face. He was drooling! I held it out to him, but before he could take it from me I snatched it back. "But..." I said teasing. "First, you'll have to give me something."

"Anything!" said Esau. He couldn't keep his eyes off the stew. I knew he wasn't thinking properly. Thinking isn't one of his strong points.

I held the stew right under his twitching nose. "I'll give you this if you let me have your special blessing and give me all the things that go with being the eldest," I said.

I took one step backwards, and waited for him to thump me, because he's like that. But what he did next surprised me even more.

Esau licked his lips. He looked at me, and he looked at the stew. "OK, it's a deal," he said. "Now give me the stew."

"Really?" I asked. "You mean it?" My heart was thumping away like mad in my chest, and my hands were shaking.

"Yeah," he said. "I said so, didn't I? Now give me something to eat."

I gave it to him as calmly as I could, but I couldn't believe it! I'd been half joking. I'd been winding him up. But Esau had taken me seriously. He really thought I meant it. Esau had given me his birthright! It was like he'd given up being the eldest son – and given the position to me. And he'd done it so easily, too.

I walked round behind one of the tents. I didn't want anyone to see me.

"Yes!" I shouted to the sky and I clenched my fists. "YES!"

"What are you doing?"

I spun round. I could feel myself going

red. It was Mum. I wondered how long she had been watching me.

"Nothing," I lied.

"Jacob," she said sternly. "I know when you're up to something. What was going on between you and Esau back there? Now tell me... I might be able to help."

That was true. I'd always had a sneaking suspicion that Mum didn't like Esau very much, either. But you can't really ask, can you? I mean mothers are supposed to love their children, aren't they?

Anyway, I knew that she would find out all about it before long. She has an uncanny knack of knowing exactly what's happening, so what was the point of hiding it from her? I might as well tell her. It's odd, but even though I'm a young man, I always feel like a little boy when I speak to Mum. So I told her everything. I told her about the stew, and I told her about Esau giving up his rights as the eldest.

"Well done!" she said slowly, when I had finished speaking. "Well done." And she smiled a funny smile to herself. She looked really quite pleased. She turned to go.

"Don't make a big thing of it, Jacob," she said. "Just wait. Your time will come.

Remember what Esau gave you today, and wait and see what will happen. Be patient. Your time will come."

Good old Mum. She surprises me sometimes. I thought she might have told me off. I know I shouldn't really have asked Esau to give me everything in exchange for some stew. My stew is good, but it's not that good! I'd tempted Esau to do something wrong. Well, stupid anyway. And stupid just about sums Esau up. I wondered what God thought about it all. But I didn't worry for too long. After all, Esau didn't have to do it. I didn't make him. He did it himself. It wasn't my fault. Esau could easily have told me what I could do with my stew! He's good at telling me what to do.

The stew! Suddenly I remembered that I'd left the pot on the fire. The whole thing was ruined, just a hard black lump in the bottom of the pot, and the fire had gone out.

I tipped some water into the pot and left it to soak. Now I was starving. I grabbed a cheese, and cut off a chunk. What a surprise, I thought to myself. I wonder what will happen next?

I remembered Mum's words. I'd just have to wait and see.

Chapter Two

The years passed. We moved around a bit, pitching our tents in new places whenever we needed to find good grazing for the flocks. Well, we didn't actually pitch the tents ourselves – the servants did that. Some people might think it's a funny way to live, being on the move most of the time. But I suppose I'm used to never settling in one place for long.

We haven't always been nomads. My grandfather, Abraham, was brought up in Ur and that's a very posh city. But it's all because of him that we lead this sort of life. You see, he believed that God told him to come and live here in Canaan. He also believed that God had promised to do something special with our family, though I've never really understood what. We seem just the same as everybody else. Very, very ordinary. Nothing special.

We've moved around to avoid famine. And always we dig wells. Each time we go to a new place, Dad insists that we dig a well. Water is what we need to survive.

As for me and Esau, we didn't get on any better. And from my point of view, there was one good thing. Esau fell right out of favour with both Mum and Dad. He got married, you see.

I know! There's nothing wrong with getting married, and we've all got to do it some time. And I know Esau got married twice – but that's pretty usual around here. Nobody thinks anything of it. Most men have more than one wife. None of that was a problem. The problem was who he married.

He married a Hittite woman! A Hittite – can you believe it?! And then he married another Hittite woman! He made the same mistake twice. Everybody knows the Hittites don't believe in God like we do. Anyway Mum and Dad didn't like Esau's wives at all. And even Dad seemed to have gone off Esau. It was as if he were disappointed in him. But Esau didn't seem to care. Anyway it was too late. He'd done it.

"Why couldn't you have married someone who believes in the Lord God?" wailed Dad.

Actually I was quite worried about Dad.

We've never been really close, but I didn't like to see him looking so old. He didn't go out much those days, and he could hardly see. He was almost blind.

I wonder what'll happen when Dad dies, I thought. Esau will be head of the family. A cold chill spread over me, and I shivered.

Suddenly I felt a hand grab me from behind. I swung round, ready to lash out. Perhaps it was a robber? Or some bandits, maybe?

"Shh!"

It was my mother Rebecca.

"What the...?" I began.

She held one finger across her mouth, grabbed me by the other hand, and pulled me into her tent. She pushed me to one corner, and I sank to the ground. Then, making sure that we were alone, she lowered the flap of the tent.

"What's going on?" I gasped.

"Listen carefully, Jacob," whispered Mum. She sat down on the floor beside me. "I've just heard your father talking to Esau. He's going to give him his special blessing. We've got no time to lose."

"What do you mean?" I asked Mum. I had no idea what she was talking about.

"Think back!" she snapped. "Remember the lentil stew – how Esau gave up everything to do with being the eldest to you?"

"Oh that!" I said. "Of course I do! But it didn't really mean anything, did it? Esau's still the eldest. He was born before me. I can't do anything about it now, can I?"

"Of course you can!" said Mum crossly. "Just listen to me, will you? I know exactly what we must do."

She leaned closer and began to whisper in my ear.

And the things I heard her say made my hair stand on end.

"Esau's just gone out hunting for some game," Mum whispered rapidly into my ear.

"So?" I asked. "What's new?"

"Be quiet!" she snapped. "I've just heard Isaac telling him to go and hunt for some game, so he can cook him his favourite meal. After they've eaten, your father will give Esau his special blessing. So, this is what we must do..."

"What do you mean?" I asked. "What can we do?"

"Plenty, Jacob," she said, and she began to explain.

I listened as Mum told me her plan. My mouth opened wide. I could hardly believe my ears. She's incredible! But now I know how she knows everything. She *listens* to other people's conversations! No wonder she was whispering now.

"So," she said, "do you understand what you've got to do?"

I nodded. I couldn't speak. She waited for me to repeat what she had just said. She wanted to make sure I understood her plan. I took a deep breath. "I'll go and choose a couple of goats from the herd, and you'll cook them in a way that Dad likes. Then I take the food to Dad, and pretend to be Esau, and Dad'll give me his blessing."

I almost chanted it. I felt like I was in a trance. I was numb. My mother had just thought of the very worst, sneakiest trick imaginable – and I was going to do it! I could hardly believe I was saying the words.

"Exactly," said Mum.

"But Mum!" I exploded and then lowered my voice. "Dad will be able to tell straight away that I'm not Esau. It will *never* work. He may be blind, but as soon as he lays a finger on me he'll know it's me. Look at me! Esau is covered in hair, and my skin's as smooth as a pebble. And Dad can't give me his blessing without touching me, can he?"

I was almost shouting by now. It was a mad idea. It would never work. Whatever had got into Mum's head?

"I've thought of that!" she spat. "I've thought of everything! I said that I would help you get your father's blessing, and I will."

"But... but... Mum," I stammered, "if Dad realises what I've done, he'll end up by cursing me, not giving me his blessing."

I felt a coldness come over me. There's

nothing worse than a father's curse, is there?

"Don't worry about that!" Mum was beginning to lose her temper. "If he curses you, then I'll say it was my fault and take the curse instead. Now why don't you just do as you're told?"

Chapter Three

I wasn't happy. I walked through the herd of goats, looking around for a couple of good young ones to cook for Dad's special meal. I had a sinking feeling that what I was about to do was very, very wrong. But I couldn't do anything about it, could I? Mum is a very strong woman, and I learned years ago that there's very little point in arguing with her.

No, I wasn't yet happy, but I *was* excited, if you know what I mean. You see, for years I'd had all these thoughts going round my head. I'd lie awake at night and plot and scheme, and think of all sorts of ways I might get one over Esau. Oh, I'd got the better of him a few times before. He may be big and strong, but he doesn't think much. I was always thinking, what if...? And now it had happened. An opportunity had fallen into my lap. It was exactly what I had been waiting for. And it seems like Mum had been waiting, too. I wondered whether she lay awake at night, plotting like me.

I bet she does, I thought. It must run in the family.

I got the goats ready and gave them to her. The pot was already on the hearth. The water was boiling and the herbs and spices were ready. She'd also made some bread.

She put the meat into the pot, and added the other ingredients.

"Stay here," she ordered. "I've got some things to get ready."

I did as I was told. But I couldn't keep still. I was pacing. I kept looking out towards the horizon, wondering how Esau was getting on. Had he caught anything yet? Was he on his way home? Would he get to Dad before me? Unlikely, but you never know.

At least Esau is so big you can see him coming a long way off, I thought to myself.

I tried to avoid looking towards my father Isaac's tent. It made me feel uncomfortable. I thought of the frail old man, lying on a stack of pillows, unaware of the trick I was about to play on him. I could feel my heart beating faster, just at the thought of it.

Well, it won't all be my fault, I thought. Esau did give up everything to me, so I'm only really taking what is mine, anyway.

And Mum seems to think it's a good idea.

But the thought didn't really make me feel much better. I felt sure that God wouldn't see it in the same way.

I saw Mum slip out of Esau's tent. She jerked her head towards her tent, and I left the cooking pot and followed her.

"Try these on," she hissed, shoving some clothes at me.

I held them out and looked at them. They were Esau's best robes. They were made of finely spun wool, brightly coloured. Not that Dad would be able to see them. But he would be able to feel them. He'd know that they were Esau's, just by the touch. I made a face. They smelled of Esau, too.

"They'll be far too big," I whispered.

"Just put them on," said Mum.

She grabbed them off me, and threw the tunic over my head.

I felt just like a little boy. I wished she wouldn't do things like that! It's embarrassing.

I pulled the tunic over my own clothes. It wasn't too big.

I looked down at my hands. I had Esau's clothes on, I was dressed up like him, I even smelled like him, but there was no getting away from it, my skin was not like Esau's in any way. Esau is hairy. Dad would only have to touch my hand, and he'd know straight away who I was.

"This isn't going to work," I said, looking at Mum. It was a stupid idea.

"Yes it is," she said firmly. "Come here."

She had some goatskins in her hand. She yanked my head down and tied a skin around the back of my neck. Then she tied some smaller pieces around both my hands.

"Believe me," she said. "This will work."

I nodded. I felt an idiot, but I suddenly knew that she was right. Wild as it was, I knew that this *was* going to work. It wasn't just that I would get so much more when Dad died, I just knew that this was really important and that somehow this blessing was very special. Yes, it was definitely worth a try.

Mum lifted up the flap of the tent. She looked about and disappeared round the corner.

A few minutes later, she returned, carrying the pot of stew and the loaf of bread.

She gave them to me.

"I've done my bit," she said slowly. "I told you that I would help you. Now it's over to you."

Chapter Four

Slowly, I walked outside. My heart was pounding inside my chest, and my mouth was dry. I could feel my mother's eyes watching me from behind, willing me to keep going. I cast a glance out to the horizon, half expecting Esau to come leaping towards me. But there was nothing.

The pot was hot and difficult to carry. The goatskins on my hands didn't help.

Please may none of the servants see me, I thought to myself.

What would I say if I saw one? "Don't mind me. I just felt like wrapping myself in goatskins and wearing my brother's clothes for a while. You really ought to try it some time!"

But I was lucky. There was no one about. Everywhere was still and quiet.

I lifted the flap of my father's tent, and stood in the entrance, letting my eyes get used to the dim light.

I could see Dad, lying in the far corner.

He was asleep. His mouth was open. He was snoring.

Perhaps I could just leave the food and run? I could tell Mum that I hadn't been able to wake Dad and that we'd have to think of something else, wait for another opportunity.

But I knew that there would never be another opportunity. Not like this one. It was now or never.

I cleared my throat.

"Father?" I said. "Dad?" My voice sounded strange.

I saw Dad move. He raised his head towards me.

"Who's that?" he asked. I could tell he was straining to hear, by the way he held his head. "Which of you is it? Esau or Jacob?"

I gulped. This really was it.

"Esau!" I said in a gruff voice, trying to sound as much like Esau as I could.

Dad paused. I didn't want to go any nearer until I absolutely had to.

"I've done just what you told me to," I said, waiting for Dad to say something.

I waited for him to say that I wasn't Esau, but Jacob. Then I'd tell him that I'd been joking and that of course I was Jacob.

But Dad didn't say anything. He was waiting, too. Perhaps he really does think I'm Esau, I thought.

I stayed near the door and continued.

"I've been out hunting, just like you asked me to," I said, rather too quickly, "and I've managed to get some of your favourite meat. I've cooked it. Can't you smell it? It's delicious!" I felt myself relax. It was working. I was beginning to get into the swing of it. "Come and eat some and then you can give me your blessing!"

"But you've done it so quickly!" said Dad, sitting upright. "However did you manage it?"

My stomach turned over. Crafty old man! He was suspicious, after all. Not even Mum had anticipated that.

I felt my mind racing with possible reasons why I had managed to hunt, kill and cook everything so quickly. But there was only one reason I could give. Only one reason which Dad would not question. In fact, he would be pleased to hear it.

"The Lord God made it possible for me," I said, still holding the pot. "He provided everything I needed and so it didn't take long at all."

I watched the old man nod his head. He was smiling. I knew he'd be pleased.

"Come here, Esau!" said Dad. "Let me touch you."

I made myself walk across the floor of the tent. It was just as well Dad was blind. He couldn't see how much I was shaking.

I could feel myself sweating underneath the goatskin around my neck. I put the pot down, by the bed, and knelt down beside Isaac.

Here goes! I thought to myself.

"Are you really Esau?" asked Dad.

"Yes!" I said. But my voice sounded just like a squeak.

I watched as Dad reached out his gnarled old hand. He moved slowly. He felt my hands, running his twisted fingers over the goatskin. I held my breath. I didn't dare move. But I was shaking inside.

"You sound just like Jacob," he muttered to himself. So I hadn't fooled him, after all. "But these are Esau's hands! I'd know them anywhere!"

I didn't risk speaking again. I just nodded, hoping that he would feel the movement, as he reached out his hand and touched my head.

"Are you really Esau?" he asked.

How many times? I thought to myself. But I didn't want to say much. Just in case.

"Yes, I am," I said as confidently as I could.

It's difficult to sound confident when your teeth are chattering.

"Bring me the food," said Dad.

I let out a silent sigh and ladled some of the food onto a dish. I guided Dad's hand towards it. I really didn't want to touch him too much. He still might guess the truth.

I poured a cup of wine and passed it to him. I watched him put the cup to his lips and take a big gulp.

Come on, Dad, I felt like saying. Get a move on. I'm in a hurry.

He wiped his mouth with the back of his hand.

"Let me bless you, Esau," he said. "It is time for me to give you my special blessing."

At last! About time! I don't think I could have stood it much longer.

Dad held out his arms and I walked towards him, letting him hug me. I felt him take a deep breath and knew that he was smelling my clothes. Not such an old fool,

27

after all. I sank to my knees and felt his
hands resting on my head.

"May the Lord God bless you," he said. A
shiver ran down my spine, and I felt a red hot
glow well up inside me. His hands felt heavy
on my head and I suddenly realised that what
Dad was doing could never be undone.

"May you be greater than your brothers,"
he said. "May those who curse you be
cursed, and those who bless you be blessed."

It was over. I'd got it! I'd got my father's
blessing.

As quickly as I could, I left the tent and
ran.

Chapter Five

I thought I saw Esau as I ran to my tent, but I put my head down and kept on running.

I punched the air. I felt as though I had won a race. I felt great – on a real high. I was buzzing all over with excitement. I'd done it! I'd really done it. Mum had been right. It had worked. I'd got my father's blessing and nobody could take it away from me. Never! Not even Esau! Especially not Esau!

"Gotcha!" I hissed, smiling, between clenched teeth.

And then I heard it. It was a loud noise, which sounded like a piercing cry of pain and a scream of fury. And I knew it was Esau.

As quickly as I could, I left my tent and ran to my mother's. I knew that even Esau wouldn't dare come in there without being invited.

Rebecca was waiting for me. She looked pale and not nearly as sure of herself as she had been a few hours earlier.

"Esau knows!" she cried, pulling me into her tent. "I watched him as he came home from hunting, and I watched him as he cooked his food. He looked so pleased with himself! Then I stood here and waited while he went into your father's tent. I suppose you heard him?" She looked up at me.

I nodded.

"Well, he's out to kill you. He says that he will wait until your father has died and then he'll get you!"

I remembered how frail Isaac had looked. He's not got long, I thought. And then I will be dead, too.

"We shouldn't have done it," I said, beginning to panic. "What's the point of having Dad's special blessing if I'm dead?"

"Listen to me," said Mum urgently. "Do what I tell you."

"Ha!" I said. "This is the second time today that you've told me what to do – and look where it's got me."

"Be quiet!" snapped Mum. "Pack some things, and go and stay with my brother, Laban, in Haran. When Esau's calmed down, I'll send you a message and you can come back home. But hurry! You've no time to lose!"

Chapter Six

There was no need to say anything else – I hurried. Well, I know what sort of temper Esau's got, don't I? He always has had a short fuse. It's that red hair of his.

Anyway, I stuffed as much as I could into a bundle. I found a good-sized water bottle too and filled it up. I picked up the remains of the loaf of bread Mum had cooked earlier and put it in the bundle. Who knows when I would have another decent meal?

I'd no idea how long it would take me to get to Haran or what I'd meet on the way. All sorts of dangers, I thought. I might not even get there. I was never the one for the outdoor life, but at this moment staying at home was probably far more dangerous than the 400-mile journey which lay ahead of me. I remembered that my grandfather, Abraham, had left Haran to settle here. Now I was making the same journey in reverse. Except my grandfather didn't have an irate brother after him.

I was all ready to go when I stopped to think about Dad. I wondered how he was feeling about it all.

It suddenly struck me that he wanted to give Esau his special blessing because he knew that he didn't have long to live. He was so frail and so weak, he couldn't possibly last much longer. And I realised that I might never have the chance to see him again.

I was making my way towards the doorway, when I heard Dad's voice. He was calling for me. "Jacob! Jacob!" he croaked.

It felt really spooky, as if he had known that I was coming to see him. I walked straight on in.

"Yes Dad," I said. I wondered whether he was going to lose his temper with me and tell me off for what I'd just done. I would not have blamed him.

But he didn't. He just beckoned me over with his long, bony finger.

I let him run his hand around my face, over my smooth skin. He took both my hands in his.

"Jacob!" he said.

"Yes Dad," I replied. I knew he wasn't going to get angry. I could tell by the look on his face.

"May the Lord God bless you," he said.

I felt a cold shiver run down my spine again, just as it had when Dad had blessed me before. I felt a gentle puff of wind on my face, and that red hot glow well up inside me. I wanted to shake. But this time it wasn't because I was afraid, scared that I was going to be found out. It was something else. But I didn't know what. It just felt weird.

"Don't marry a Hittite woman!"

said Dad. I smiled to myself. He was still hung up about Esau's wives. "Marry one of your Uncle Laban's daughters. And may God bless you and give you lots of children, just as he promised to me and your grandad."

He held his hand on my head. I felt it pressing down on me like a weight. I wanted to go, but I knew that I'd just have to wait until he had finished.

Odd the way things work out, I thought. Here I am, ready to escape from home, running away from my brother who has threatened to kill me, and now my father is giving me another blessing, even though I've just played a huge trick on him. And all he's bothered about is who I'm going to marry! You never can tell how things will work out.

Anyway, at that moment marriage was the last thing on my mind.

I just wanted to get out of there alive!

Chapter Seven

I was exhausted. It had been a long day. A lot had happened and my whole life had changed. I knew that I'd got a long way to go before I reached my Uncle Laban.

I'd no idea how far I'd travelled. Mum had pointed me in the direction of Haran, and I'd just kept on heading north. At first it had been fairly easy, but it wasn't long before the countryside changed.

Alone, I had time to think. I was lonely. I wasn't used to being on my own. At home there were always plenty of people bustling around. If you got fed up with your family you could go and talk to one of the servants. There was always someone. But now I had no one. I wondered if I would ever see my family again – not that I wanted to see Esau again in a hurry. But it was odd. I'd done everything to get Dad's special blessing, but being blessed hadn't done me much good, so far!

The sun began to set and I felt cold.

In the distance I saw some almond trees. A wave of relief swept over me. I'd already reached Luz. It's amazing how a death threat can make you move!

I tethered my donkey to one of the trees and began to unpack. I was glad that I had had time to bring bread and water with me. I was starving.

I spread my cloak out on the ground and found a smooth flat stone for a pillow. There's nothing worse than sleeping with your head on the ground at night, is there? In the morning your hair is full of dew, and what with the damp and the cold, you're bound to have a stiff neck and a thumping headache.

I was exhausted. I lay down and wrapped myself in my cloak. I looked up at the sky. There were hardly any clouds. The moon shone above me and there were hundreds of stars twinkling over my head. I tried to count them, but there were far too many. Looking at them made me think.

I thought about God and how he had made the world. Funny really, but I was thinking about God quite a lot. I remembered something that my grandfather Abraham had said. The Lord God had shown him the night sky, full of stars, and had promised that he would have as many people in his family as there were stars in the sky.

My eyes felt heavy and my feet ached. Before long I sank into a deep, dark sleep.

All of a sudden a loud noise startled me and I sat bolt upright.

A brilliant light shone in my eyes.

"What the...?" I stammered.

The clouds parted and a gigantic ladder tumbled down from the sky and landed beside me..

The light was hurting my eyes. Suddenly I saw a strange figure on the top of the ladder. He began to climb down, making his way towards me.

I couldn't move. I tried to move my feet, but they seemed rooted to the ground. I gulped. Then I saw another figure, and another, moving steadily down the ladder.

"Help!" I wanted to cry. "Stay away from me!"

But just like my feet, my tongue was paralysed and I couldn't make a sound.

I watched, unable to do or say anything, as the figures moved down the ladder.

As my eyes grew used to the brilliant white light, I saw that the figures were not unlike men. And yet their eyes shone and their faces glowed, and on their backs they had wings.

The strange figures moved effortlessly down the ladder, almost gliding their way to the bottom.

I don't mind telling you, I was scared. In fact, I was petrified. But I couldn't do anything about it. I just watched anxiously to see what would happen next.

As the first figure reached the bottom rung, he didn't get off and come towards me. Instead, he began to climb up again into the sky, until he reached the top of the ladder.

There's another world up there, I thought.

I began to relax. I watched as the strange beings moved up and down. It was quite the most amazing thing I'd ever seen.

I might as well enjoy it while I have the chance, I thought.

I heard a loud thundering noise, coming from above my head. I held my hands over my ears and looked up.

From the top of the ladder I saw another figure, a figure made of fire. It sparkled and shone and glittered, surrounded by a blinding brilliance.

Wow! I thought. Who in the world is that?!

And then I knew. I knew exactly who this incredible, amazing person was, even though I had never seen him before. There was no other explanation. If that's heaven, I thought, still staring upwards, then those must be angels, and that must be...

I had hardly said the word when I found I had sunk to my knees. I just couldn't keep my eyes off the face at the top of the ladder.

I felt his eyes looking deep into mine, staring at me.

"I am the Lord God," spoke the figure. "In the past, I have spoken to both your grandfather and your father," said God, his voice sounding like a thundering waterfall, ringing in my ears. "I made them both a promise. And now I will make the same promise to you. I'm going to give you and your family the land you are lying on. Your family will be great, as numerous as specks of dust and your descendants will spread throughout the whole world!"

Wow! I felt my stomach leap with excitement. Dad had told us that God had made him a promise and now I was hearing it with my own ears!

But he hadn't finished. "I also promise that I will stay with you and look after you wherever you go. I won't ever leave you. I'll make sure that what I've said comes true."

I felt God's words echoing in my head, until they grew to a loud crescendo. Then they slowly grew fainter and fainter until there was silence. As I stared into heaven, the brilliance faded, until it finally disappeared, covered by the inky blackness of the night. And yet...

I rubbed my eyes, and stretched. I stared up at the sky. It was still dark.

Then a thought struck me, and a cold

shiver ran down the length of my spine, tingling my toes and the back of my neck.

I'd been asleep. What I'd just seen was a dream, only a dream!

I stared about me, into the shadows of the night.

The Lord God must be here, I thought, as I looked up at the stars. I'd better watch out! I know for sure that God has been here tonight!

I felt afraid. Really, really scared.

I'd no idea that God could do that – talk to you in your sleep! Dad had told me he'd spoken to God and that God had spoken to him and that my grandfather Abraham had done it too. But Dad could be a bit weird at times, and I'd never heard God speak myself.

But now I'd heard the voice of God – and seen him! I'd never thought much about God before although he must have been watching me all the time! And from now on, I wouldn't be on my own. God had promised to look out for me.

Chapter Eight

I didn't go back to sleep. I mean, nobody would be able to, not after a dream like that.

I lay there, staring up at the sky until the stars began to fade and the darkness changed to grey and the orange glow of the sun came up over the hills.

By the time it was day, I'd had an idea.

I didn't think that I would ever forget that dream, but it's funny the things you forget, even really important things. That dream was one of the most important things that had ever happened to me. I mean, it's not every day that a ladder comes down from the sky and you can glimpse a corner of heaven, is it? Never mind hearing the voice of the Lord God! I wanted to do something special to remember my dream. After all, it had been quite amazing, and this was a remarkable place.

I looked about to see what I could do. But there wasn't anything much. Just the almond trees.

Then I spotted the stone I'd used as a pillow. It was much bigger than I'd remembered it being last night. In fact it was really heavy.

I picked up the stone and made it stand upright, so that it looked a bit like a pillar.

I scrabbled about in my bundle of stuff until I found a small bottle, full of olive oil. I poured the oil over the top of the stone as an offering to God.

I think that if I'd had more time – and the things to work with – I might have made an altar. I remember that was the sort of thing

Grandad Abraham used to do after he'd spoken with God.

I looked up at the morning sky and cleared my throat. Well, God had promised to watch out for me, so I guessed that he was doing exactly that, even though I couldn't see him. All the same, I felt a bit strange talking to him. I wasn't used to talking to God, was I?

"Lord God," I said, looking up to the sky. I rather wondered whether his face would appear in the clouds, but it didn't. "You've promised to look after me, and I know that you've been here, so I've put up a stone, as a sort of sign to say that you were here."

I hesitated for a moment and looked around. It was a lonely place, miles from anywhere, but from now on I knew that it would always be special. I cleared my throat and looked at the morning light.

"And... um... I think I'll call this place something different. I think I'll call it Bethel, which means 'God's house' because you've been here."

I don't know why I was telling God that! I mean, he already knew, didn't he?

"And," I took a deep breath, "because you've made a promise to me, I'm going to make one to you. I'm going to give you a tenth of everything I have from now on. I promise."

Nothing happened. Nobody spoke. I must be cracking up! I'm speaking to a stone! I thought to myself, as I packed up my things.

But deep inside, I knew that I hadn't been speaking to a stone at all. I had been talking to the Lord God – and what's more, I knew that the Lord God had heard me!

Chapter Nine

Water!

I don't know how long I'd been travelling. I'd sort of lost track of the days. But it was a very, very long time since I'd left home.

At first I'd thought a lot about Mum and Dad. I still did. Especially whether Isaac was still alive, although I didn't really want to think about that too much. I felt really gutted every time I thought about my family.

I also wondered about Esau. Occasionally, if I heard a loud noise, or something gave me a fright, I'd wonder if Esau was about to leap on me from behind. But I'd stopped looking over my shoulder every few minutes a long time ago.

I was fed up with travelling. My donkey was, too. The bundle in which I'd put my stuff when I left home was very much smaller and lighter now. There was virtually nothing in it. Nothing to eat, anyway. I'd done a bit of hunting to get fresh food, and

I'd bought some things from passing traders. And several people had been kind to me and given me a meal and something to drink.

But now I wanted to get to Uncle Laban's and settle down for a bit. I wanted to have a decent meal and something to drink. Something like lentil stew, although I wasn't sure whether I would ever be able to eat lentil stew again without feeling guilty. I just wanted to stop. I was so tired of being on the move. I must be near Haran now.

The sun was burning down and the ground was hot. I was parched. When I saw the well I cheered up. There was a massive stone over the top of it, and lots of sheep had gathered around, waiting for it to be opened up, so that they could have a drink. I couldn't wait to have a drink, either. I licked my dry lips and thought about the cool, clear water.

I saw some shepherds walking towards the well.

"Hi!" I said.

"Hello," they replied. I could tell straight away that they were from the north. I wondered if they could tell me exactly where I was. I hadn't got a clue.

"Where are you from?" I asked.

"Haran," they replied.

"Wow!" I said. "That's where I'm going. My Uncle Laban lives there. Do you know him?"

"Yes," they replied. "Look over there and you'll see his daughter, Rachel. She's coming to give her sheep some water, too."

The shepherds pointed in the distance and I saw a young woman walking towards me.

Amazing! Not only had I found water, exactly when I needed it, but I'd accidentally bumped into my cousin Rachel.

Suddenly I got that strange tingling feeling, like fingers pattering down my spine and that deep, hot glow came up from inside me again. This was an amazing coincidence. But perhaps it wasn't a coincidence at all; perhaps this was what the Lord God meant when he said that he'd watch out for me.

The tingling sensation stopped and I jumped back to reality. Rachel was almost at the well.

Without thinking, I ran towards her and pushed away the huge stone at the top. I surprised myself. I didn't know I was so strong.

Rachel looked at me and smiled. I smiled
back, but I felt a lump rise in my throat.

"Hello," I said. "I'm your cousin Jacob."

I felt really awkward. I didn't know what
to say. I knew that I sounded completely stupid. But Rachel didn't seem fazed at all. It
was as if she was always bumping into long-
lost cousins by the side of the well.

And the really, really embarrassing thing
was that I felt tears welling up in my eyes. I
don't know why. I haven't cried for years.

But I felt so happy that I just had to cry. I couldn't stop myself.

I think it was because of all the scheming and plotting, tricking Dad, cheating Esau, running away, being scared, feeling exhausted – and now the relief of finally getting here and finding Laban's family so easily. And Rachel was so pretty. Her face was so kind. It just made me want to cry.

What a weirdo she'll think I am, I thought.

But she didn't seem to mind.

"I'll go and tell my father you're here!" she said, and she ran off towards the town in the distance.

I watched her go and took a long, cool drink.

And then I had a funny thought. Out of the blue, I suddenly remembered what my Dad had said about getting married!

Chapter Ten

"Well, haven't you grown!" roared Uncle Laban, slapping me on the back. "Look at you! Rebecca's little boy! How the years have flown. Now sit down and tell me everything. I want to know all about it."

It was easy talking to Uncle Laban. He was so like my mother it was uncanny. It wasn't just the way he looked; it was the way he listened and the way he spoke. You could tell he was thinking all the time – just like my mother.

Anyway, he was great. He made me feel really welcome. "You're one of the family, Jacob," he said. "Stay here. You can help with the sheep."

At last I could relax. And I worked. I worked really hard, actually. And do you know? I began to enjoy being outdoors. I took the sheep further and further away from the tents, looking for new pastures.

And of course there was Rachel. Wow! She was beautiful, and she was really nice with it. I felt sorry for her older sister, Leah. It must be hard having such a lovely little sister. She was OK – but nothing special. Not like Rachel.

I tried to stop thinking about her. There was no point. I hadn't any money, and I hadn't any prospects. I was just a family guest. There was no hope. I'd never marry Rachel.

One day Uncle Laban asked to see me. I wondered what he was going to say. I hope he's not going to tell me to leave, I thought. I really didn't fancy being on the road again, and anyway I hadn't got anywhere to go.

"You've been working very hard, Jacob," said Laban. "Everyone can see that. And I don't think it's fair that you're doing all this work for nothing. So... tell me how much you think I should pay you."

"Actually," I said, taking a deep breath. "I don't really want any money – well not at the moment, anyway. What I want most of all, in the whole world, is to get married to Rachel, and I know I'm not much of a catch. I haven't any money; I haven't got anything that I can give you, or her. So..."

I paused for a moment to have a look at Laban's face. But he didn't interrupt me. "I'll work for you for seven years. You won't have to pay me anything. But when the time's up, I want you to let Rachel be my wife."

I could tell exactly what Laban was thinking. He nodded his head and smiled. "It's a deal!" he said. "You work for me for seven years and then you can marry Rachel."

He clasped my hand, and threw his other arm around my shoulder. Then he went off whistling to himself.

I let out a deep breath. "Phew!" It had been a long shot; but it had worked. I was going to marry Rachel! I couldn't wait.

But I'd have to. I'd have to wait seven years. I watched Laban weave his way through the flock of sheep. And it suddenly dawned on me how easy it had been to strike a deal with him to marry his beautiful daughter. He hadn't put up any argument at all. Not one little objection. It was all a bit fishy. But anyway, I'd got what I wanted.

Sly old fox! I thought, still watching Laban's back. I bet he knew what I was going to ask, all the time.

Seven years is a long time by anyone's calculation. But the years passed very quickly.

It was just as well, really. It helped because I was so busy. I worked and worked, looking after the sheep, helping to build up Laban's flocks and herds. He became a rich man.

It gave me time. Time to think, time to get to know Rachel better, and time to change. Some people only meet for the first time on their wedding day. Imagine that! What a shock it must be. At least I wasn't going to have a shock like that.

I knew I'd changed quite a bit since I'd left home. There'd been no word from my mother, so I hadn't gone back. This was my home – for the moment, anyway. I wondered what had happened to Esau. I wondered if he'd found a wife that our parents approved of. I knew they'd approve of Rachel. Everyone did – you couldn't help it.

But it was odd, getting married and not having my parents or my brother there. Still, I suppose Laban was my uncle as well as my father-in-law to be. He was family, after all.

At long last our wedding day arrived. The invitations had been sent out and the food cooked. The musicians arrived and the special wedding canopy put up, all ready for Rachel and me to sit underneath. We were going to have a great time. I was really excited. I had been waiting such a long time.

That evening I walked with some friends to collect Rachel. This is the custom of my people. Guests joined us on the way. Everyone was smiling and laughing.

"He's here! He's here!"

We could hear the excited cries coming from the house long before we got there.

Then the door slammed shut.

We stood outside in the dark. The door of the house opened slowly. I just held my breath.

Rachel came out of the house, wearing the most beautiful dress. In the golden lamplight she looked wonderful. Her wedding veil hid her face, but I could imagine her smile. I hoped she was feeling as happy as I was.

There were bridesmaids everywhere! Rachel was surrounded by them. As we set off, all the guests were holding torches, and everything looked magical in the flickering light and the moonlight.

Time passed in a haze. We ate, we drank, we danced and we sang. We laughed and we told stories. Finally, when everyone was exhausted, we went our separate ways, and my bride and I went to our tent.

The next morning, I woke early and watched the light change as the sun came up. I felt really happy. It was great the way things had turned out. I had finally landed on my feet.

"Morning."

"Good morning!" I replied, still smiling. I turned my head in the direction of the voice.

"What the...?" I stuttered, grabbing the covers up to my throat. It was Leah. "You must have got the wrong tent."

"No," she replied, looking at me with those watery eyes of hers. "This is *my* tent."

"I don't think so," I said as politely as I could, trying to sit upright, while still hanging on to the covers. "This is my tent... Well, mine and Rachel's tent, so if you don't mind..."

"Actually," said Leah walking towards me, "it *is* my tent. *Yours* and mine. In case

57

you didn't know, you married *me* yesterday, not Rachel. I'm your wife!"

I sprang to my feet and grabbed my tunic.

"Wait here," I hissed at Leah.

I marched out of the tent.

"Where's Laban?" I roared. "Where is he?"

I didn't wait for him to ask me in. I just went.

"What have you done?" I screamed. "You lying, cheating, scheming, twisted..." There were not enough words to describe how I felt about him. I could have done him some serious damage. But I didn't. I just looked him in the eye and waited to hear what he had to say.

"Jacob!" he said, trying to smile. "Jake! Be reasonable. Listen to me. I can understand why you're feeling a little upset..."

"A little upset!" I spat.

"And perhaps I should have told you first..."

"That would have been nice!" I said sarcastically.

"But the thing is... You see, Leah *is* older than Rachel..."

"So...?"

"So," continued Laban, "it just isn't done

for a younger sister to get married before her older sister. It's just not what we *do* around here..." His voice faded away.

I loosened my grip on his tunic.

"Well, you could at least have told me first," I said. A wave of anger swept over me. "I've worked hard for you for seven years so I could marry *Rachel*, not Leah. And you've just lied and cheated and twisted things to suit yourself. You've even cheated your own daughters! How could you do this to your own family?"

"You tell me," said Laban slowly, the corners of his mouth curling upwards into a sly smile. "You should know."

I clenched my fists and then let go of him.

Of course, he was right. I was something of an expert in cheating members of my own family. And now it had happened to me, and I didn't like it at all.

"Well, yes," I said. "But it's still no excuse for what you've done."

Laban nodded. "I think we can come to some agreement," he said. "Finish off the wedding celebrations this week, and then at the end of the week you can marry Rachel."

"Agreed," I said.

"And then," said Laban, "after you've

worked for me for another seven years, you'll be free to go."

Too right, I thought. I'll have worked for you for fourteen years for nothing – although I will be married to Rachel.

The thought of marrying Rachel cheered me up a bit.

But I'll never trust Laban again, I thought.

Chapter Eleven

It wasn't a very good start, I can tell you. In the space of a week, I hadn't just got one wife – I'd got two. Not that there was anything wrong with having two wives – but wives who are sisters is not a good idea. Everybody knows that. Especially when you love one and you don't particularly like the other. It wasn't at all like I'd imagined it to be.

But that wasn't the end of it. Leah had baby after baby, all of them fine strapping sons. And Rachel didn't seem able to have any children at all.

Things got more than a little tense at times, as I'm sure you can imagine. I mean, I knew exactly what it was like not to get on with my brother, and Rachel and Leah didn't get on either. They were always having a go at each other, mainly about the children. And I was stuck right in the middle.

In the end I got quite cross with Rachel. She knew that I loved her and I didn't love

Leah, but she was so jealous.

"I can't help it!" I shouted at her. "It's up to God who has children or not – not me!"

Funnily enough, not long after that, Rachel became pregnant. She had a little boy called Joseph. But even then she wasn't really satisfied.

"I hope God gives me another son!" I heard her say.

Anyway, what with Rachel and Leah at each other's throats and the children, and the fact that I didn't really trust Laban any more, I thought it was time that we moved on.

I wanted to go home, back to Canaan. I kept thinking about that weird dream I'd had when God had spoken to me, and every time I thought about it, I got these funny feelings, running up and down my spine.

Those feelings also told me that leaving was the right thing to do. After all, Canaan was the place that God had promised to give me when he spoke to me at Bethel, and he couldn't give it to me while I was stuck in Haran, could he?

To have land of my own might make all the difference, and might help calm the situation between Rachel and Leah. At least then I'd have something to give to my children. And even though things had got a bit messy on the home front, I still knew that God was watching over me.

I waited for a good time to speak to Laban. By then I only spoke to him when I absolutely had to. I didn't trust him at all. I'd seen him at work, and I knew from first hand what it felt like to be the victim of one of his plans. He only looked after his own interests.

I also knew that he was involved in things which wree not quite right. He tried to find out what would happen in the future. He swirled his wine in his divining cup, and watched the patterns form. I didn't feel comfortable about it. It didn't seem right.

"Let me go," I said to Laban one day. I came straight to the point. "I want to take my family back to Canaan."

He looked a bit shocked. But I was wary. "I've worked very hard for you," I said, "and now I want to go."

"But I don't want you to go," he said. "My daughters, my grandchildren..."

I managed to stop myself saying anything. I knew he didn't really care about anyone, other than himself.

"Look," he continued. "If I have shown you any kindness at all, please don't go..."

I could feel myself softening. Although I distrusted him, Laban was still a likeable rogue. He had taken me in when I was desperate and treated me like one of his own children – not that that meant anything, in the end.

"Actually," he said, "something very strange happened to me the other day.

"I was looking at my divining cup, swirling the wine, looking to see the patterns form from the sediment at the bottom, and suddenly I saw it!"

"Saw what?" I said.

"You!" said Laban.

"Oh yes!" I said. He'd have to do better than that.

"I did!" said Laban. He looked really serious. "I saw you at the bottom of my cup, and I saw all the good things that have happened to me since you arrived. And then I knew that the Lord God has blessed me and given me good things, not because of me, but because of you."

He paused a moment. "I need you to stay. I'm asking you to stay... Please."

"But everything I've done since I've been here has been for you," I said slowly. "Your flocks have increased, and you've got more wealthy. I need to do something for me. I've got my own family now, you know."

"So, what do you want?" asked Laban. He was the sort of person who was always trying to strike a deal.

This time I'd thought ahead and I knew for the first time ever that I was one step ahead of Uncle Laban.

"Nothing," I said. That made him look up. "I'll carry on as usual, looking after your sheep and goats, but let me keep all the ones that are speckled or spotted and the same with the black lambs. Let me be paid in speckles and spots!"

"Done," said Laban, grinning broadly. "You can have what you want."

"Thank you," I said, smiling as well. And I knew exactly what he was thinking. Laban thought I was a fool. He thought he wasn't really giving away anything.

But I knew otherwise, as he'd just have to wait and see.

Chapter Twelve

It wasn't really a trick, honest. But it did work. You see, I'd heard other shepherds talk about it before. There's this theory that whatever a sheep or a goat sees affects them in some way. I know what you're thinking! It's all an old wives' tale. Well, perhaps it is, but God was on my side, so listen to what happened.

That day I watched as old Laban sorted through his flocks. He was so thorough – and crafty! First of all, he gave his sons the speckled sheep and goats and the dark-coloured lambs and sent them miles away to graze. He left the rest, completely unmarked, for me. He thought he'd beaten me.

As soon as I'd found some good grazing, I got hold of as many twigs and branches as I could find. There were lots of trees about – almond, plane and poplar. Then I peeled back the bark, so that the branches were striped, and placed them by the water troughs because that was where the animals mated.

Don't ask me how, but it worked! The animals saw the stripes when they mated, and before long they gave birth to speckled, spotted or dark-coloured young ones. I made sure that only the strongest and the healthiest ones saw the branches, so I soon built up a fine flock of my own, making sure I kept my animals well away from Laban's plain-coloured.

"Your cousins are saying you're a thief!" one of the men told me. "They've heard you're stealing Laban's flocks."

"Rubbish!" I said sharply. "I haven't done anything wrong, only what we agreed."

But I knew it meant trouble. Laban and his sons had been looking for a fight for a while. They had treated me unfairly, and now they were getting what they deserved.

Looks like I'm going to be on the run again! I thought as I tried to sleep. I'd got so much on my mind that I didn't expect to sleep at all.

But as soon as I lay down, I felt my eyes grow heavy and a great inky blackness swept over me.

"Jacob!"

I heard a voice and I struggled up. I knew I'd heard it somewhere before, but I couldn't quite remember where. I woke up, my heart thumping.

"Jacob!"

I looked about, but I couldn't see anyone.

"Yes," I said. "I'm over here."

Perhaps there was something wrong with the sheep. It was the breeding season after all. Just my luck, after things had been going so well – on the animal front, anyway.

Then the voice spoke again, and I felt the same warmth welling up inside me.

"I am the Lord God," said the voice.

"I spoke to you at Bethel, many years ago. I made you a promise, and you made one to me."

A picture suddenly flashed into my mind. I saw Bethel, and the ladder, and the angels, and I remembered the stone I had put in place.

"Jacob," said God, "go home to your hown family and I will bless you."

Brilliant! What timing!

I tried to speak, but as I did so, I suddenly woke up!

Wow! I'd had another dream. I thought back to what God had said. There was no time to lose. I was on the move again. I had to get out of there!

But this time it was different. I *knew* the Lord God was watching over me.

I sent for Leah and Rachel.

"Look, I know he's your father and this is your home, but we've got to get out of here!"

Leah and Rachel looked at me. So did the children. I hadn't been looking forward to saying all this, but we had to get going. I didn't really want to discuss it.

"Yes," said Leah.

"I agree," said Rachel.

You could have knocked me over. This was a first! My wives actually agreed about something!

"Dad's cheated us and he's cheated you," said Leah. "He's got what he deserves."

"We must do whatever God has told you," said Rachel.

"But don't tell Laban!" I warned.

"He'll come after us," said Rachel. "I know he will. He'll try and find us by any means. I bet he even uses his divining cups or his teraphim to find us – unless we stop him!"

Rachel was probably right. I knew Laban was into those things. He spent a lot of time looking into his special divining cups, trying to see pictures as he swirled the wine around.

Then there were the teraphim. They were the sort of things that the Canaanite people worshipped. They didn't believe in the Lord God. They had idols made of wood or stone, big and small. Laban said that some of them looked like our dead relatives, but I wasn't so sure. They didn't look like anyone I'd ever known. And I couldn't see much point in asking them for advice. After all, they were dead.

All that stuff gave me the creeps. But I'd just have to leave Laban to do whatever he was going to do. There was no time to stop him.

We packed quickly. I made sure my flocks went on ahead, and I got some camels for Rachel and Leah and the children, and sent them off in the right direction. The servants would have to walk.

It was amazing how much stuff I'd got, considering I'd arrived with virtually nothing. I needed more than a couple of bundles slung onto a donkey now. Actually, that cheered me up a bit. I wasn't going back to Canaan empty-handed. I'd got sheep and goats, wives and children and servants. And all the tents for us to live in. I'd done quite well for myself.

Chapter Thirteen

A week later and I thought we'd got away with it. We'd got to Gilead which was great. There was plenty of good grazing for the flocks, but it was hilly, which slowed us down a bit. So it seemed like a good place to stop and make camp.

I was wrong.

"What have you done?" roared Laban. "Why have you tricked me?"

I glanced quickly about. I could hardly believe it! Not only had Laban caught us up, he'd overtaken us, and had made his camp right in our way, blocking our only escape route. We were surrounded.

"You should have told me you were leaving! I'd have thrown a party for you!"

I didn't know whether he was being sarcastic or not, but I thought it best not to say anything.

Laban took one step closer to me. I could see his eyes flashing in anger. His nostrils flared as he spoke. I braced myself, ready to

fight. I suddenly thought of Esau. I really
didn't want to fight the old man, but if he
went for me I'd have to.

"You didn't give me a chance to say good-
bye to my daughters or my grandchildren. I
could kill you..." His voice trailed away.

I gulped and sweat broke out on my forehead. I'd no doubt he could. But I wasn't
going to let him try. I clenched my fists,
ready to strike.

"But I can't!" he said. "Last night I had a very strange dream. The Lord God told me not to say anything good or bad to you. So, I can't. I won't."

I let out a long sigh and relaxed my fists slightly. Whatever Laban said, he still looked angry.

So, I thought, I'm not the only one God speaks to in dreams.

I wondered whether Laban got the same strange sensation that I did when God was speaking. I wondered whether his spine shivered and his body glowed. But now was not the time to ask.

"What I don't understand," he said, still angry, "is why you've stolen from me. Why have you stolen my teraphim, my lucky charms? I need them, you know. I want them back."

I was so surprised I didn't know what to say. "I haven't!" I said at last. "I didn't run away from you because I had stolen anything from you – especially your teraphim. Feel free. Search the place. You won't find them here."

I watched as Laban rushed into Leah's tent. He came out some time later, and shook his head.

"Well?" I asked.

"Nothing," he replied.

He made his way towards Rachel's tent, and I followed.

I watched as he searched the tent, moving mats, clawing through bundles. Rachel was lying down. She didn't move, she just watched her father.

He soon gave up the search. There was nothing to be found.

"Satisfied?" I asked. It was my turn to be angry. I could have grabbed him by the throat, but I didn't.

"Now you tell me – what have I done wrong? You've hunted me down like a criminal and you've turned everything upside-down. What have you found? Nothing! I've worked hard for you for twenty years – and all you've done is trick me and lie to me! If you could have got away without giving me anything you would have done. But God has seen how you've treated me – that's why he spoke to you last night, in your dream!"

Laban didn't say anything. He just looked at me. He nodded his old, grey head.

"Everything you've got was mine," he said sadly. "Your wives, your children, and your flocks. We mustn't fall out. We must come to some agreement."

Not another deal! I thought, but I nodded my head at the same time.

"Look after my daughters," said Laban.

"I will," I said.

I saw a large stone. It reminded me of the stone I had put into the ground at Bethel. I dragged it over and put it into the ground.

"This stone will be a sign of our friendship," I said.

"Agreed," said Laban. "I promise not to go past it, to get my own back on you. You promise the same."

"I promise," I said.

We parted the next morning. We were friends.

I didn't find out until later that Rachel had taken the teraphim. She'd been lying on them!

I don't know why she thought we'd need these ridiculous lucky charms. Maybe she thought her father wouldn't be able to find us without them. Well, she was certainly wrong there! Anyway, I made a mental note to sit down with my family and tell them more about my God, the one true God, and his promise to go with us and protect us.

Chapter Fourteen

Just when you think everything's been sorted, something else happens, doesn't it?

I thought that everything would be fine now, and that we could just head on back for home. But in my anxiety to escape from Laban I had allowed myeslf to forget about Esau.

The last time I had seen him, he had been very, very angry. So angry, in fact, he wanted to kill me, tear me limb from limb. I couldn't imagine that much had changed.

"Let's send him a message," I said, thinking quickly. I realised that if I was going to settle in my homeland, then I would first have to make peace with my twin brother. "Tell him that I would *love* to see him. Tell him that I *respect* him a lot. Tell him that I think of myself as his *servant*. Tell him that I have been staying with my Uncle Laban for all these years, and that I now have a family and riches of my own... Assure him that we come in peace."

The messenger came back, much too quickly.

"Well?" I snapped. "What did he say?"

"He's coming to meet you... and he's bringing four hundred men who'd like to meet you too!"

"Four hundred men..." I felt sick. "Four hundred..."

The messenger nodded.

There was no escape. It was obvious. Esau was out to get me. And not just me, but my family and all my flocks and herds as well.

I couldn't help but smile. It was quite funny really, in a very strange way. You think you have got away with something, but years and years later, it all catches up with you.

I could think of only one thing to do. "Separate everything and everybody into two groups!" I ordered. At least if Esau attacked one group the other might escape.

I don't have to tell you how scared I felt. Scared with a capital S. So scared that it was all I could do to stop my teeth chattering and my hands shaking. I hadn't felt as scared as this since I had tricked Esau and run away from home.

But this was scarier! I mean, in a way,

I deserved it. But my family didn't. Neither did my servants – nor the sheep nor the goats. But they were all in it with me – right up to their necks.

I took some time out, on my own.

"Lord God," I shouted. "You promised to look after me. You made the same promise to my father Isaac, and my grandfather Abraham. And you were the one who told me to go back to my own country – and now look what's happened!"

I paused for a moment. There wasn't a reply. But I was sure God was listening.

"I'm sure that Esau is out to kill us all. You have been so good to me. You have looked after me. I know I don't deserve anything! But please save me! Keep the promises you made to me and my family. Please!"

Nothing happened. God didn't reply. Silence.

Now what shall I do? I thought. I had only one idea.

I spent the night choosing my best sheep and goats – and my best camels and cattle.

"Take these animals to Esau," I said to my servants. "Say that they are a present from me. Tell him that I'm coming to see him... a bit later...!"

I watched as my servants disappeared over the horizon, taking my best animals with them.

Probably the last time I see them! I thought to myself.

But then, what use are camels and goats to a dead man?

Night came. I knew I wouldn't be able to sleep. I was a condemned man. I just wanted to be alone.

"Go across to the other side of the River Jabbok," I said to Rachel and Leah. "Take everything with you. You'll be safe there."

They didn't argue. They just packed. Even the children did as they were told. They could tell it was serious.

I watched as my family and all my things disappeared into the darkness. I heard the sound of the water as they crossed the river. Then there was silence. I wondered if I would ever see them again.

I sat, huddled up, alone.

I was surrounded by darkness. It was so still and quiet. Peaceful almost. At least it would have been if I hadn't felt so afraid. I looked up at the stars, twinkling in the sky, and tried to count them. I thought back to the time when I'd tried to count them before, and I remembered the promise God had made to Grandad Abraham.

Suddenly, I thought I saw something move. I froze in terror, staring into the inky blackness. I stared as hard as I could, and then I saw it. Something was moving in the darkness. I scrambled to my feet. I did not look away, but kept staring at the same spot, trying to make out who or what it was.

"Who's there?" I whispered.

There was no reply.

I screwed up my eyes, trying to see more clearly. There was definitely someone out there, and they were getting closer.

The figure moved slowly towards me and as it got nearer I could see it was a man.

Had Esau crept out at night to hunt me down? My heart thumped wildly in my chest.

"Who are you?" I shouted.

But my voice just echoed in the darkness.

"I know there's someone there!" I cried. "Tell me who you are!"

But before I could speak another word,

two hands grabbed me. Their pincer-like grip dug deep into my flesh and I struggled to get free.

Chapter Fifteen

I gasped for breath. I could hardly breathe.

For one moment I thought the man would completely overpower me.

Then, using all my strength, I pushed myself forwards and into him. I held onto the man's arms and braced myself against him. I looked into his face, and in the darkness I knew that I had never seen him before. It was not Esau. It was a stranger.

And yet there was something about him that I recognised.

I felt the stranger's muscles flexed against me. I knew that he was stronger than I was. He was stronger and tougher than any man I had ever seen.

And suddenly I realised that I didn't want to give up. I wasn't going to let him win. I wasn't going to let him beat me.

The Lord God had given me his promise. He had promised things to me and to my family. He'd promised to give us lots of children. He'd promised to give us our own land. He'd promised to make us into a great nation. He'd promised to stay with me. And although I didn't know where he was now, I had this strange feeling that he was with me. I suddenly knew that I was not going to let this stranger snatch everything God had promised away from me. My family was only the start of all that God had promised. If I lost, I would lose everything, not just for me but for my children and their children.

Something clicked inside me, and I knew I had a chance. I was not going to give up.

We stayed locked together. Each time the stranger moved, I moved with him, determined not to let go.

Sweat poured off my body, and I knew that the ground under my feet was wet, making my feet slip and slide.

My muscles shuddered, aching with pain, and my hands and fingers lost all feeling. But I did not loosen my grip.

Slowly the darkness began to fade, and the golden light of dawn shone over the horizon.

Had I really been wrestling half the night with this stranger?

I relaxed my grip for a moment. The man lunged forward and with one great blow struck me on the hip.

I felt the bone shoot out of the socket, and I cried out as the pain shot through my body. But I did not let go.

Then, for the first time, the man spoke. "Let go of me," he said. "The night is over. It is morning."

And then I knew. I recognised the voice. It was the voice I had heard speaking to me from heaven. It was the voice I had heard in my dreams. It was the voice of the Lord God.

"I won't let you go!" I said bravely. "Not until you bless me!"

"What's your name?" he asked.

"My name? He knows my name!" I thought.

"Jacob!" I gasped, still refusing to let go of him.

"No it isn't!" said the man. "Not any more! I'm giving you a new name. Your name will be Israel, because it means that you have struggled with God and with men, and you have not given up!"

"Tell me *your* name!" I whispered, slowly letting my aching hands relax their grip of the man's arms.

"Don't you know who I am?" the main replied.

I knew I didn't have to ask. I knew that I was speaking to the Lord God.

I sank to my knees, exhausted. I knelt before the man's feet. I felt his hands resting on my head.

"I will bless you, Israel," he said. "I will keep my promises to you."

A fire burned through my body and the feelings that I'd had before ran up and down my spine. But the feeling was greater, and it consumed my whole being. I knew that something amazing was happening to me. It was as if I was being cleaned by the heat of the flames. And I knew that whatever happened I would never be the same again.

Then, as suddenly as he had come, the man disappeared.

I was alone.

I have seen God face to face! I thought to myself. I have struggled and wrestled with him. And I'm still alive!

Every part of me throbbed with pain. I wanted to rest.

But there was no chance of that! As I looked up, I saw something that made me clamber to my feet.

Chapter Sixteen

Four hundred men were marching steadily towards me. Four hundred and one.

I could tell Esau anywhere. And I knew who he was, even when he was a long way away. He looked older, but he also looked stronger and tougher. I wondered how I looked to him. A limping old wreck, I suppose.

I recognised the way he walked, the way he swung his arms, and the way he held his head.

There was no way out. And I was far too tired to fight.

I limped towards Esau. Each step I took sent a sharp searing pain through my body. "God is with me," I said to myself. "He's made promises to me. He will not let me down."

It seemed like the longest walk of my life.

But I just kept looking at Esau. I kept on walking towards him.

How I'd changed! I was still afraid,

but this time I wasn't going to run away. Well, I couldn't, anyway. But I didn't want to. I wanted to face him. I wanted to speak to my brother, my twin.

It was odd, but inside I felt quite calm. Normally, my mind would have been racing, plotting and thinking up ways to get out of this. But I'd no tricks left. They didn't work, anyway – not in the end.

I stopped walking. Esau wasn't far away. I stopped and bowed down before him. I bent to the ground, ignoring the pain, once, twice, seven times, as if he was a king. I'd done him wrong and I knew it. But God was with me.

Esau could do what he liked now. There was nothing I could do.

I waited, staring at the ground. I waited to hear Esau shout. I waited to hear the cries of his men as they ran towards me, ready to hack me to the ground.

But there was only silence.

Suddenly, I heard the sound of running. I looked up to see what was happening.

Esau was running towards me. But he didn't have a sword in his hand.

As he ran towards me, our eyes met. Tears trickled down Esau's face. He threw his arms around me, and hugged me!

"Jacob!" he said. "Jake!"

"Esau!" I cried. "My brother."

It's strange really, but for the first time in my life, I knew I loved my brother. Well, we're twins – and even though we're not identical, we've got a lot in common.

It's odd the way things work out. Not at all like you expect. I thought back to all the things that had happened to me. Right back to the time when I made that lentil stew and saw my chance to trick Esau out of his inheritance. I don't know what I expected to happen then, but I certainly never thought I would see a ladder of angels in a dream, or wrestle with God, or see his face and live.

And then I realised I'd changed. God had given me a new name, and I'd changed inside. God had made promises to me, and he had kept them and I'd made promises to him. God had been with me all the time, and I knew that he would stay with me and my family in the future.

Who knows what will happen in the future? I don't. But I do know that I left home with nothing, and I came home with wives and children, sheep and goats. God had given me so much. And as we pitched our tents and made our home in Canaan, I built an altar to honour the Lord God, who had been with me through thick and thin.

If you've enjoyed this book, why not look out for...

'I didn't feel nervous because I knew that I was doing what the Lord God wanted and he was the one who was really in control. "This is it!" I shouted. My voice boomed across the mountain. "People  of Israel, from today you will have to decide who you are going to worship – God or Baal. We'll ask both of them to send down fire from heaven and the true God is the one who sends down fire!"

Elijah tells us what it was like to be one of God's prophets when Queen Jezebel was determined to kill him. At times he was running for his life. But whenever Elijah felt very alone, God had already got a plan in place.

ISBN 1 85999 452 0

Available from your local Christian bookshop

Suddenly the boat lurched sideways and the ropes of the nets creaked and groaned. 'Fish!' yelled Andrew, trying to tug the nets in. 'Help me, Peter!' I grabbed the net and heaved as hard as I could. I felt the boat drop in the

water. We slowly made our way to the shore and the waiting figure of Jesus. He looked so ordinary, just like one of us. And yet I knew he wasn't ordinary at all.

Peter tells us what it was like to leave fishing and follow Jesus as one of his disciples. There were good times and bad times – like the time he let Jesus down. But even after that, Jesus still had a job for Peter to do.

ISBN 1 85999 453 9

Available from your local Christian bookshop

'Looks can be misleading, can't then? I mean, you can look at a person and think how cool and calm they are. But that's not always right, is it? Take me, for instance. I know that I look strong and tough. I look like a leader, which is just as well really, because that's what I am. But inside it can be different, scary even.'

Joshua tells us what it was really like to change the Israelites – a bunch of grumblers – into a lean, mean fighting machine, ready to invade the Promised Land. And how God gave him the strength he needed.

ISBN 1 85999 451 2

Available from your local Christian bookshop

Other titles in the series

- Understanding Acupressure
- Understanding Acupuncture
- Understanding The Alexander Technique
- Understanding Aloe Vera
- Understanding Aromatherapy
- Understanding Bach Flower Remedies
- Understanding The Bowen Technique
- Understanding Craniosacral Therapy
- Understanding Echinacea
- Understanding Fish Oils
- Understanding Garlic
- Understanding Homoeopathy
- Understanding Head Massage
- Understanding Kinesiology
- Understanding Massage
- Understanding Reflexology
- Understanding Reiki
- Understanding St. John's Wort
- Understanding Shiatsu
- Understanding Yoga

First published in 2006 by First Stone Publishing
PO Box 8 Lydney Gloucestershire GL15 6YD

The contents of this book are for information only and are not intended as a substitute for appropriate medical attention. The author and publishers admit no liability for any consequences arising from following any advice contained within this book. If you have any concerns about your health or medication, always consult your doctor.

ISBN 1 904439 55 1

Printed and bound in China through Printworks International Ltd.